I0530165

Now What?

THE LOGICAL AND PRACTICAL WAY TO SOLVE ANY CHALLENGE

GINO POMILIA

BRITON

Briton Publishing, LLC
810 Eastgate North Drive, Suite 200
Cincinnati, OH 45245

Copyright 2025 Gino Pomilia. All Rights Reserved.

No part of this publication may be reproduced in any form, or by any means, electronic or mechanical, including photocopying, recording, or any information browsing, storage, or retrieval system, without permission from Briton Publishing.

ISBN: 978-1-956216-23-3

Briton Publishing, LLC Books are distributed by Ingram Content Group.

For my son J.D.

You have faced many difficult challenges in your life, and you have always had the quiet courage to meet them head-on. With each of these challenges, and the uncertainties that come with them, I have watched you navigate your way and come out on the other side of each, stronger and more confident. You have developed into one of the finest young men that I have ever encountered in my entire lifetime, and in the process, you have remained true to yourself as a man, a husband, and a father. I am so very proud that you are my son, and I am so very honored that you have become my closest friend, whom I trust with my life.

Contents

Foreword by Chad Kreuter

I lived with Gino the summer after I graduated high school, before heading off to Pepperdine. I didn't officially play for him, but we spent hours training, working out, and having real conversations about life. That time had a huge impact on me — not just as an athlete, but as a young man.

Gino is like a father to me. He's someone I've always looked up to. The way he leads, teaches, and connects with people has stuck with me through my playing career and my years coaching in professional baseball.

When he told me that some of this book was inspired by our time together, it meant a lot. But if you know Gino, you know he's been inspiring people for a long time — he just has that kind of presence.

This book is Gino — straightforward, honest, and full of wisdom that pushes you to stop making excuses and start moving forward. If you're facing a challenge, this will help you get back on track.

And if you really want to see Gino light up, just mention Elvis Presley. He'll grab a mic and break into an Elvis song without missing a beat.

Chad Kreuter is a former Major League catcher with a 19-year professional playing career, including 16 seasons at the Major League Baseball (MLB) level. He played for teams including the Dodgers, Tigers, Rangers, and White Sox. After retiring, he spent 20 years coaching professionally with roles at USC, the New York Mets Organization, and others. Chad is known for his leadership, player development, and a deep understanding of the game, both on and off the field.

Foreword by Buddy Biancalana

Now What? is a book from which any human can benefit, not from just reading it, but by taking the action steps on each page.

I have known Gino since being coached by him at Redwood High School in Larkspur, CA. I've watched him for decades achieve his every desire as he moved through the obstacles that come with being human. His "can do" attitude is displayed throughout this book, and these words are not just rhetoric, but will lift and energize the reader to take action and dismantle any resistance to moving life challenges. This is a book that should be picked up and looked at every day, in order to receive its full benefit.

Buddy Biancalana is a Kansas City Royals World Series Champion, Founder of Zone Motion, and co-author of "7 Secrets of World Class Athletes."

Introduction

Throughout my entire career, I have been a baseball coach, both on the high school and collegiate level, which now spans over 30 years. In 1986, I was coaching what was to be the number-one high school baseball team in the state of California. During that time, one of my best players, who was hoping to get a college scholarship, was pressing and pretty much just thinking about himself. Because of this approach, he was receiving poor results.

At the beginning of the season, he had struck out two times in a row in a single game. When he came back to the dugout, feeling sorry for himself, he said, "Coach, I can't hit this pitcher. All he's doing is throwing me curveballs." I informed my player that what the pitcher was doing was perfectly legal. I then informed him that his attitude had now pretty much determined his success, or lack thereof, because he had convinced himself that he could not hit this pitcher. Therefore, I told him that he would be sitting on the bench for the remainder of the game. He was shocked! He was a captain, and I loved this young man. He was even more shocked when I benched him the next game (I knew that the team was good enough to be successful during this little experiment.) I told him that I was not going to put him back into the line-up until I was convinced that he was ready to be successful.

During the next few days at practice, he would come early and stay late, hardly saying a word. He worked extra hard, putting in extra time, and working on hitting the curveball. I continued to give him encouragement and guidance when it was called for, as long as I knew he was listening and adjusting; however, he was on a "Personal Mission."

When the next game came around, he came up to me and said: "Coach, I don't care what position I play or where I hit in the line-up. I just want to get back in the game, and I will hit whatever this damn pitcher throws over the plate." My response was simple: "Now, you are ready to play."

He enjoyed the rest of the season, never realizing that he had led the entire league in hitting with a .471 batting average. How did he get to this place? He realized the "challenge" and knew that no one else was going to solve it for him. He realized there was only one way to solve the problem, and that was for him to adjust, figure it out, and persevere.

This young man did end up getting a college scholarship, and when he came across a difficult situation, he knew that the answer lay within his own thoughts, attitude, and ability. When he graduated from college, he had set eight team records.

We all come upon situations in our lives that are not going the way we hoped, and this happens to EVERYONE. The answer is NEVER to complain to someone else, but to seek the answer and learn by devising some type of plan that comes from within ourselves. We learn to trust the person we see in the mirror. We learn to trust our own instincts and thus grow to learn that we all have the ability within ourselves to be successful at overcoming personal challenges.

Lastly, is this easy? No, not at first. It's not supposed to be easy, but the good news is, IT GETS EASIER.

~Gino Pomilia

About the Author

Gino Pomilia was born in San Francisco, and all 4 of his grandparents were Italian immigrants.

He was the first of his generation of 36 first cousins to graduate from college, and he did so without any financial help from his parents. This, however, created quite a barrier between his father and himself, who wanted him to work in the family business, so things between them were either awkward or silent. No longer allowed to work in his father's restaurant, Gino did many things, including cleaning toilets, to achieve a college degree. Once successful as both a teacher and a baseball coach, setting various winning records, his father finally, publicly, claimed Gino as his son.

Gino has been a teacher and a coach for over 35 years, on both the high school and collegiate levels, and he runs yearly baseball camps in Marin County, California. He also invented and patented the Easton Thunderstick, a hand-eye coordination training bat, used in batting practice. He has competed over 25 times in the World Championship Ride & Tie, a cross-country endurance running and horseback riding event, and he has finished in the "Top Ten" 12 times. He has also performed as Elvis Presley, on various occasions, stating that he was not really sure how good he was, but in his mind, he was amazing.

Gino currently lives in the Lake Tahoe Basin with his wife Julie, who is a granddaughter of Roy Rogers and Dale Evans. She has written two books of her own: *Your Heroes My Grandparents* and *Roy and Dale On Stage and In Between*. Together, they have two Palomino horses, a pony, a miniature donkey, and four Border Collies. Their blended family, at the moment, has 4 children and 6 grandchildren.

Lastly, Gino believes that whatever determination and strength he possesses today has come from his mother, Gloria.

Let's Get Started!

> "Great minds find solutions.
> Weak minds find excuses."
> Eleanor Roosevelt

The Challenge:

_____

_____

_____

_____

_____

_____

_____

_____

_____

_____

_____

_____

_____

_____

_____

Now What?

_____

_____

_____

_____

_____

_____

_____

_____

_____

_____

_____

_____

_____

_____

_____

_____

"What would you attempt, if you
knew you would not fail?"
Eleanor Roosevelt & Robert H. Schuller

The Challenge:

_____

_____

_____

_____

_____

_____

_____

_____

_____

_____

_____

_____

_____

_____

_____

Now What?

_____

_____

_____

_____

_____

_____

_____

_____

_____

_____

_____

_____

_____

_____

_____

_____

> "Many times, we tell ourselves we can't do something until we do it."
> Unknown

The Challenge:

_____

_____

_____

_____

_____

_____

_____

_____

_____

_____

_____

_____

_____

_____

Now What?

_____

_____

_____

_____

_____

_____

_____

_____

_____

_____

_____

_____

_____

_____

_____

"We start today from where we are right now."
Author, Gino Pomilia

The Challenge:

Now What?

_____

_____

_____

_____

_____

_____

"No one ever accomplishes
anything by giving up."
Words attributed to Dan O'Brien

The Challenge:

Now What?

_____

_____

_____

_____

_____

_____

_____

_____

_____

_____

_____

_____

_____

_____

"Many successful ideas usually
follow many unsuccessful ideas."
Author, Gino Pomilia

The Challenge:

_____

_____

_____

_____

_____

_____

_____

_____

_____

_____

_____

_____

_____

_____

_____

_____

Now What?

_____

_____

_____

_____

_____

_____

_____

_____

_____

_____

_____

_____

_____

_____

_____

_____

"Wise people learn whenever they can; fools learn only when they must."
Duke of Wellington

The Challenge:

_____

_____

_____

_____

_____

_____

_____

_____

_____

_____

_____

_____

_____

_____

Now What?

_____

_____

_____

_____

_____

_____

_____

_____

_____

_____

_____

_____

_____

_____

_____

_____

_____

"People will do when they have to."
John, Chef from Dominic's Restaurant

The Challenge:

Now What?

_____

_____

_____

_____

_____

_____

_____

_____

_____

_____

_____

_____

_____

_____

_____

_____

_____

_____

_____

_____

_____

_____

_____

_____

_____

_____

_____

_____

_____

_____

"If you want to accomplish something that you've never accomplished before, you must be willing to do things that you've never done before."
Thomas Jefferson

The Challenge:

_____

_____

_____

_____

_____

_____

_____

_____

_____

_____

_____

_____

Now What?

_____

_____

_____

_____

_____

_____

_____

_____

_____

_____

_____

_____

_____

> *"Failures are stepping stones to success."*
> Ancient Chinese Proverb

The Challenge:

_____

_____

_____

_____

_____

_____

_____

_____

_____

_____

_____

_____

_____

_____

Now What?

_____

_____

_____

_____

_____

_____

_____

_____

_____

_____

_____

_____

_____

_____

_____

> "You will fail at everything that you
> do not attempt."
> Author, Gino Pomilia

The Challenge:

_____

_____

_____

_____

_____

_____

_____

_____

_____

_____

_____

_____

_____

_____

_____

_____

Now What?

_____

_____

_____

_____

_____

_____

_____

_____

_____

_____

_____

_____

_____

_____

_____

_____

_____

"Failure is not the opposite of
success; it is part of success."
James Clear

The Challenge:

_____

_____

_____

_____

_____

_____

_____

_____

_____

_____

_____

_____

_____

_____

_____

Now What?

_____

_____

_____

_____

_____

_____

_____

_____

_____

_____

_____

_____

_____

_____

_____

"Life is tough, but it's tougher
if you're stupid."
John Wayne

The Challenge:

Now What?

_____

_____

_____

_____

_____

_____

_____

_____

_____

_____

_____

_____

_____

_____

_____

"Forget the mistake. Remember the
lesson."
Anonymous

The Challenge:

_____

_____

_____

_____

_____

_____

_____

_____

_____

_____

_____

_____

_____

_____

_____

_____

Now What?

_____

_____

_____

_____

_____

_____

_____

_____

_____

_____

_____

_____

_____

_____

_____

> "If you're on the wrong track, every station you come to will be the wrong station."
> Bernard Malamud

The Challenge:

_____

_____

_____

_____

_____

_____

_____

_____

_____

_____

_____

_____

_____

_____

Now What?

_____

_____

_____

_____

_____

_____

_____

_____

_____

_____

_____

_____

_____

_____

_____

_____

> "We learn from our mistakes,
> not from our successes."
> Bram Stoker

The Challenge:

_____

_____

_____

_____

_____

_____

_____

_____

_____

_____

_____

_____

_____

_____

_____

_____

_____

Now What?

_____

_____

_____

_____

_____

_____

_____

_____

_____

_____

_____

_____

_____

_____

_____

_____

_____

_____

"The only things in life that you really regret are the risks you didn't take."
Ann Margret, Grumpy Old Men

The Challenge:

_____

_____

_____

_____

_____

_____

_____

_____

_____

_____

_____

_____

_____

_____

_____

Now What?

_____

_____

_____

_____

_____

_____

_____

_____

_____

_____

_____

_____

_____

_____

_____

_____

_____

"You have nothing to lose by saying 'I can'. You have a lot to lose by saying 'I can't'."
Author, Gino Pomilia

The Challenge:

_____
_____
_____
_____
_____
_____
_____
_____
_____
_____
_____
_____
_____

Now What?

_____
_____
_____
_____
_____
_____
_____
_____
_____
_____
_____
_____
_____
_____
_____

"You have either excuses or
results, not both."
Arnold Schwarzenegger

The Challenge:

_____

_____

_____

_____

_____

_____

_____

_____

_____

_____

_____

_____

_____

_____

_____

Now What?

_____

_____

_____

_____

_____

_____

_____

_____

_____

_____

_____

_____

_____

_____

_____

_____

> "What you are not changing,
> you are choosing."
> Laurie Buchanan

The Challenge:

Now What?

_____

_____

_____

_____

_____

_____

_____

_____

_____

_____

_____

_____

_____

_____

_____

_____

> "Every path has a few puddles. Just keep moving forward."
> George Herbert

The Challenge:

_____

_____

_____

_____

_____

_____

_____

_____

_____

_____

_____

_____

_____

_____

_____

Now What?

_____

_____

_____

_____

_____

_____

_____

_____

_____

_____

_____

_____

_____

_____

_____

_____

> "The person who never attempts anything never fails. They also never succeed."
> Albert Einstein

The Challenge:

_____

Now What?

_____

"The man on top of the mountain
didn't fall there."
Vince Lombardi

The Challenge:

_____

_____

_____

_____

_____

_____

_____

_____

_____

_____

_____

_____

_____

_____

Now What?

_____

_____

_____

_____

_____

_____

_____

_____

_____

_____

_____

_____

_____

_____

_____

_____

"It's not who you are that holds you back. It's who you think you are not."
Jean-Michel Basquiat

The Challenge:

_____

_____

_____

_____

_____

_____

_____

_____

_____

_____

_____

_____

_____

_____

Now What?

_____

_____

_____

_____

_____

_____

_____

_____

_____

_____

_____

_____

_____

_____

"Inhale confidence. Exhale doubt."
Coach Al Endriss

The Challenge:

Now What?

_____

_____

_____

_____

_____

_____

_____

_____

_____

_____

_____

_____

_____

_____

_____

_____

_____

"If you want to do something bad enough, you'll find a way. If not, you'll find an excuse."
Jim Rohn

The Challenge:

_____

_____

_____

_____

_____

_____

_____

_____

_____

_____

_____

_____

_____

_____

Now What?

_____

_____

_____

_____

_____

_____

_____

_____

_____

_____

_____

_____

_____

_____

_____

"It doesn't matter how slowly you go, as long as you don't stop."
Confucius

The Challenge:

_____

_____

_____

_____

_____

_____

_____

_____

_____

_____

_____

_____

_____

Now What?

_____

_____

_____

_____

_____

_____

_____

_____

_____

_____

_____

_____

_____

_____

"Many times, the most negative voice we hear is the one inside of us. Be your own motivational coach."
Author, Gino Pomilia

The Challenge:

_____

_____

_____

_____

_____

_____

_____

_____

_____

_____

_____

_____

_____

_____

_____

Now What?

_____

_____

_____

_____

_____

_____

_____

_____

_____

_____

_____

_____

_____

_____

_____

_____

"Saying, 'I can, and I will',
can take you a long way."
Author, Gino Pomilia

The Challenge:

Now What?

_____

_____

_____

_____

_____

_____

_____

_____

_____

_____

_____

_____

_____

_____

_____

_____

_____

"Never be afraid of trying, because you may be afraid of failing. You might just succeed."
Author, Gino Pomilia

The Challenge:

_____

_____

_____

_____

_____

_____

_____

_____

_____

_____

_____

_____

_____

_____

_____

Now What?

_____

_____

_____

_____

_____

_____

_____

_____

_____

_____

_____

_____

_____

_____

_____

"Be willing to take the first step in your own life. Don't wait for others to do this for you."
Author, Gino Pomilia

The Challenge:

_____

_____

_____

_____

_____

_____

_____

_____

_____

_____

_____

_____

_____

_____

Now What?

_____

_____

_____

_____

_____

_____

_____

_____

_____

_____

_____

_____

_____

_____

_____

_____

"Whenever you feel like giving up,
think of all the people that would
love to see you fail."
Unknown

The Challenge:

_____

_____

_____

_____

_____

_____

_____

_____

_____

_____

_____

_____

_____

Now What?

_____

_____

_____

_____

_____

_____

_____

_____

_____

_____

_____

_____

_____

_____

_____

> "Failing is a part of life. Not trying
> again is a choice."
> Words attributed to Confucius

The Challenge:

_____

_____

_____

_____

_____

_____

_____

_____

_____

_____

_____

_____

_____

_____

Now What?

_____

_____

_____

_____

_____

_____

_____

_____

_____

_____

_____

_____

_____

_____

_____

_____

"Never let yesterday affect today."
John Wayne

The Challenge:

Now What?

_____

_____

_____

_____

_____

_____

_____

_____

_____

_____

_____

_____

_____

_____

_____

_____

_____

"Fear is the enemy of logic."
Frank Sinatra

The Challenge:

Now What?

_____

_____

_____

_____

_____

_____

_____

_____

_____

_____

_____

_____

_____

_____

_____

"Everybody is a work-in-progress."
Joe Filice

The Challenge:

Now What?

_____

_____

_____

_____

_____

_____

_____

_____

_____

_____

_____

_____

_____

_____

_____

_____

_____

_____

_____

_____

_____

_____

_____

_____

_____

_____

_____

_____

_____

_____

_____

_____

"You never know how strong you are, until being strong is the only choice you have."
Bob Marley

The Challenge:

Now What?

_____

_____

_____

_____

_____

_____

_____

_____

_____

_____

_____

_____

_____

_____

_____

_____

_____

_____

_____

_____

_____

_____

_____

_____

_____

_____

_____

_____

_____

_____

_____

> "Good things come to those who wait, but only those things left from those who hustled."
> John Goelz, SSU Baseball

The Challenge:

_____

_____

_____

_____

_____

_____

_____

_____

_____

_____

_____

_____

_____

Now What?

_____

_____

_____

_____

_____

_____

_____

_____

_____

_____

_____

_____

_____

_____

_____

"Small changes bring big results."
James Clear

The Challenge:

Now What?

_____

_____

_____

_____

_____

_____

_____

_____

_____

_____

_____

_____

_____

_____

_____

_____

_____

_____

"It's not that I'm smart; it's just that I stay with problems longer."
Albert Einstein

The Challenge:

_____

_____

_____

_____

_____

_____

_____

_____

_____

_____

_____

_____

_____

_____

_____

Now What?

_____

_____

_____

_____

_____

_____

_____

_____

_____

_____

_____

_____

_____

_____

_____

_____

"You get what you repeat."
James Clear

The Challenge:

_____

_____

_____

_____

_____

_____

_____

_____

_____

_____

_____

_____

_____

_____

_____

_____

_____

_____

_____

_____

_____

_____

_____

_____

_____

_____

_____

_____

_____

_____

_____

_____

_____

> "Failure is the only opportunity to begin again, this time, more intelligently."
> Henry Ford

The Challenge:

_____

_____

_____

_____

_____

_____

_____

_____

_____

_____

_____

_____

_____

_____

Now What?

_____

_____

_____

_____

_____

_____

_____

_____

_____

_____

_____

_____

_____

_____

> "If you give up, you'll never be successful."
> Dan O'Brien

The Challenge

_____

_____

_____

_____

_____

_____

_____

_____

_____

_____

_____

_____

_____

_____

_____

Now What?

_____

_____

_____

_____

_____

_____

_____

_____

_____

_____

_____

_____

_____

_____

_____

_____

"You never fail, until you stop trying."
Albert Einstein

The Challenge:

Now What?

_____

_____

_____

_____

_____

_____

_____

_____

_____

_____

_____

_____

_____

_____

_____

_____

_____

_____

"You will become your habits, so
develop good habits."
Words attributed to James Clear

The Challenge:

_____

_____

_____

_____

_____

_____

_____

_____

_____

_____

_____

_____

_____

_____

_____

Now What?

_____

_____

_____

_____

_____

_____

_____

_____

_____

_____

_____

_____

_____

_____

_____

_____

"Many of life's failures are people who didn't realize how close they were to success when they gave up".
Thomas Edison

The Challenge:

_____

_____

_____

_____

_____

_____

_____

_____

_____

_____

_____

_____

_____

_____

Now What?

_____

_____

_____

_____

_____

_____

_____

_____

_____

_____

_____

_____

_____

_____

"You will miss 100% of the
shots you do not take."
Wayne Gretzky

The Challenge:

Now What?

_____

_____

_____

_____

_____

_____

_____

_____

_____

_____

_____

_____

_____

_____

_____

_____

_____

_____

_____

_____

_____

_____

_____

_____

_____

_____

_____

_____

_____

_____

_____

_____

"It always seems impossible,
until it's done."
Nelson Mandela

The Challenge:

Now What?

_____

_____

_____

_____

_____

_____

_____

_____

_____

_____

_____

_____

_____

_____

_____

_____

> "Building habits in the present allows you to do more of what you want in the future."
> James Clear

The Challenge:

_____

_____

_____

_____

_____

_____

_____

_____

_____

_____

_____

_____

_____

_____

Now What?

_____

_____

_____

_____

_____

_____

_____

_____

_____

_____

_____

_____

_____

_____

_____

_____

"A person who never made a
mistake, never tried anything new."
Albert Einstein

The Challenge:

Now What?

_____

_____

_____

_____

_____

_____

"Weakness invites wolves."
Senator John Kennedy

The Challenge:

Now What?

_____

_____

_____

_____

_____

_____

_____

_____

_____

_____

_____

_____

_____

_____

_____

_____

"It's not what you believe.
It's how hard you believe it."
From Indiana Jones and the Dial of Destiny

The Challenge:

_____

_____

_____

_____

_____

_____

_____

_____

_____

_____

_____

_____

_____

Now What?

_____

_____

_____

_____

_____

_____

_____

_____

_____

_____

_____

_____

_____

_____

_____

"What's the secret of success? *Right decisions.* How do you make the right decisions? *Experience.* How do you get experience? Wrong decisions."
John Wayne

The Challenge:

_____

_____

_____

_____

_____

_____

_____

_____

_____

_____

_____

_____

_____

Now What?

_____

_____

_____

_____

_____

_____

_____

_____

_____

_____

_____

_____

_____

_____

_____

"When 'I can't' comes upon 'I must',
then what will you do?"
Author, Gino Pomilia

The Challenge:

Now What?

_____

_____

_____

_____

_____

_____

_____

_____

_____

_____

_____

_____

_____

_____

_____

_____

_____

_____

_____

_____

_____

_____

_____

_____

_____

_____

_____

_____

_____

_____

_____

_____

> "Perfection lives in small moments."
> John Dutton, *Yellowstone*

The Challenge:

_____

_____

_____

_____

_____

_____

_____

_____

_____

_____

_____

_____

_____

_____

_____

Now What?

_____

_____

_____

_____

_____

_____

_____

_____

_____

_____

_____

_____

_____

_____

_____

_____

"99% of the failures come from people who have the habit of making excuses."
George Washington Carver

The Challenge:

_____

_____

_____

_____

_____

_____

_____

_____

_____

_____

_____

_____

_____

Now What?

_____

_____

_____

_____

_____

_____

_____

_____

_____

_____

_____

_____

_____

> "Stop making excuses and start looking for solutions."
> Stephenie Zamora

The Challenge:

_____

_____

_____

_____

_____

_____

_____

_____

_____

_____

_____

_____

_____

_____

_____

Now What?

_____

_____

_____

_____

_____

_____

_____

_____

_____

_____

_____

_____

_____

_____

_____

"With the same habits, you will end up with the same results, but with better habits, anything is possible."
James Clear

The Challenge:

_____

_____

_____

_____

_____

_____

_____

_____

_____

_____

_____

_____

_____

Now What?

_____

_____

_____

_____

_____

_____

_____

_____

_____

_____

_____

_____

_____

_____

> "There is no shortcut to
> achievement."
> George Washington Carver

The Challenge:

_____

_____

_____

_____

_____

_____

_____

_____

_____

_____

_____

_____

_____

_____

Now What?

_____

_____

_____

_____

_____

_____

_____

_____

_____

_____

_____

_____

_____

_____

_____

_____

"The most practical way to change who you are is to change what you do."
James Clear

The Challenge:

Now What?

_____

_____

_____

_____

_____

_____

_____

_____

_____

_____

_____

_____

_____

_____

_____

_____

_____

_____

_____

_____

_____

_____

_____

_____

_____

_____

"Nothing great ever started without controversy."
Author, Gino Pomilia

The Challenge:

_____

_____

_____

_____

_____

_____

_____

_____

_____

_____

_____

_____

_____

_____

_____

Now What?

_____

_____

_____

_____

_____

_____

_____

_____

_____

_____

_____

_____

_____

_____

_____

"Every action you take is a vote for
the person you wish to become."
James Clear

The Challenge:

Now What?

_____

_____

_____

_____

_____

_____

_____

_____

_____

_____

_____

_____

_____

_____

_____

_____

"If you get 1% better each day for one year, you'll end up 37 times better by the time you're done."
James Clear

The Challenge:

_____

_____

_____

_____

_____

_____

_____

_____

_____

_____

_____

_____

_____

_____

Now What?

_____

_____

_____

_____

_____

_____

_____

_____

_____

_____

_____

_____

_____

_____

_____

"There is no normal life.
There's only life."
Doc Holiday, "Tombstone"

The Challenge:

_____

_____

_____

_____

_____

_____

_____

_____

_____

_____

_____

_____

_____

_____

Now What?

_____

_____

_____

_____

_____

_____

_____

_____

_____

_____

_____

_____

_____

_____

"You're never wrong
if you do the right thing."
Mark Twain

The Challenge:

Now What?

_____

_____

_____

_____

_____

_____

_____

_____

_____

_____

_____

_____

_____

_____

_____

_____

_____

_____

_____

_____

_____

_____

_____

_____

_____

_____

> "Time goes slow for those who wait."
> Henry Van Dyke

The Challenge:

_____

_____

_____

_____

_____

_____

_____

_____

_____

_____

_____

_____

_____

_____

_____

_____

Now What?

_____

_____

_____

_____

_____

_____

_____

_____

_____

_____

_____

_____

_____

_____

_____

_____

"Americans should never be
captives of their fears."
General George Patton

The Challenge:

Now What?

_____

_____

_____

_____

_____

_____

_____

_____

_____

_____

_____

_____

_____

_____

_____

"When tomorrow comes,
don't regret yesterday."
John Wayne

The Challenge:

_____

_____

_____

_____

_____

_____

_____

_____

_____

_____

_____

_____

_____

_____

Now What?

_____

_____

_____

_____

_____

_____

_____

_____

_____

_____

_____

_____

_____

_____

> "Good judgment comes from experience, and a lot of that comes from bad judgment."
> John Wayne

The Challenge:

_____

_____

_____

_____

_____

_____

_____

_____

_____

_____

_____

_____

Now What?

_____

_____

_____

_____

_____

_____

_____

_____

_____

_____

_____

_____

_____

> "If you find yourself in a
> hole, stop digging."
> Will Rogers

The Challenge:

Now What?

_____

_____

_____

_____

_____

_____

_____

_____

_____

_____

_____

_____

_____

_____

_____

_____

_____

_____

_____

_____

_____

_____

_____

_____

_____

_____

"Most of the stuff people worry about, ain't never gonna happen."
Attributed to Mark Twain

The Challenge:

_____

_____

_____

_____

_____

_____

_____

_____

_____

_____

_____

_____

_____

_____

Now What?

_____

_____

_____

_____

_____

_____

_____

_____

_____

_____

_____

_____

_____

_____

_____

"Never fear failure. Anticipate
success."
Coach Al Endriss

The Challenge:

_____

_____

_____

_____

_____

_____

_____

_____

_____

_____

_____

_____

_____

_____

_____

_____

Now What?

_____

_____

_____

_____

_____

_____

_____

_____

_____

_____

_____

_____

_____

_____

_____

_____

> "Courage comes from living
> the life we want."
> An Old Cowboy Saying

The Challenge:

_____

_____

_____

_____

_____

_____

_____

_____

_____

_____

_____

_____

_____

_____

Now What?

_____

_____

_____

_____

_____

_____

_____

_____

_____

_____

_____

_____

_____

_____

_____

_____

"Life is like baseball; there's always another pitch coming, which means there can always be another outcome."
Author, Gino Pomilia

The Challenge:

_____

_____

_____

_____

_____

_____

_____

_____

_____

_____

_____

_____

_____

Now What?

_____

_____

_____

_____

_____

_____

_____

_____

_____

_____

_____

_____

_____

_____

_____

"No great discovery ever started off
by someone being rational."
Anonymous

The Challenge:

_____

_____

_____

_____

_____

_____

_____

_____

_____

_____

_____

_____

_____

_____

Now What?

_____

_____

_____

_____

_____

_____

_____

_____

_____

_____

_____

_____

_____

_____

_____

"Actions are remembered long
after words are forgotten."
John C. Maxwell

The Challenge:

Now What?

_____

_____

_____

_____

_____

_____

_____

_____

_____

_____

_____

_____

_____

_____

_____

_____

_____

_____

_____

_____

_____

_____

_____

_____

_____

_____

"To live the life you want makes you
successful."
John Lennon

The Challenge:

_____

_____

_____

_____

_____

_____

_____

_____

_____

_____

_____

_____

_____

_____

_____

Now What?

_____

_____

_____

_____

_____

_____

_____

_____

_____

_____

_____

_____

_____

_____

_____

_____

"It is not the mountain that you
must master. It is yourself."
Tim Nowell

The Challenge:

_____

_____

_____

_____

_____

_____

_____

_____

_____

_____

_____

_____

_____

_____

Now What?

_____

_____

_____

_____

_____

_____

_____

_____

_____

_____

_____

_____

_____

_____

_____

"When you come across tough hurdles, you can either use them to make yourself tougher, or you can use them to make excuses."
Unknown

The Challenge:

_____

_____

_____

_____

_____

_____

_____

_____

_____

_____

_____

_____

_____

Now What?

_____

_____

_____

_____

_____

_____

_____

_____

_____

_____

_____

_____

_____

_____

_____

> "Those who don't take a stand and 'sit on the fence' usually end up with a post up their butt."
> Stephen Shapiro

The Challenge:

_____

_____

_____

_____

_____

_____

_____

_____

_____

_____

_____

_____

_____

_____

Now What?

_____

_____

_____

_____

_____

_____

_____

_____

_____

_____

_____

_____

_____

_____

_____

_____

"There are two types of people: those that look at what they have and are grateful, and those that look at what they have and lament over what they don't have. The first are always happy. The second are never happy."
Author, Gino Pomilia

The Challenge:

_____

_____

_____

_____

_____

_____

_____

_____

_____

_____

_____

_____

_____

Now What?

_____

_____

_____

_____

_____

_____

_____

_____

_____

_____

_____

_____

_____

_____

> "Nothing great happens when
> you hold back."
> Scott Elrod

The Challenge:

_____

_____

_____

_____

_____

_____

_____

_____

_____

_____

_____

_____

_____

_____

Now What?

_____

_____

_____

_____

_____

_____

_____

_____

_____

_____

_____

_____

_____

"Never make permanent decisions
based on temporary emotions."
Craig Groeschel

The Challenge:

_____

_____

_____

_____

_____

_____

_____

_____

_____

_____

_____

_____

_____

Now What?

_____

_____

_____

_____

_____

_____

_____

_____

_____

_____

_____

_____

_____

_____

_____

"Only God can point the finger."
Loretta, *Moonstruck*

The Challenge:

_____

_____

_____

_____

_____

_____

_____

_____

_____

_____

_____

_____

_____

_____

_____

_____

Now What?

_____

_____

_____

_____

_____

_____

_____

_____

_____

_____

_____

_____

_____

_____

_____

> "How you do anything is how
> you do everything."
> Martha Beck

The Challenge:

Now What?

_____

_____

_____

_____

_____   _____

_____   _____

_____   _____

_____   _____

_____   _____

_____   _____

_____   _____

_____   _____

_____   _____

_____   _____

_____   _____

_____   _____

_____   _____

_____   _____

_____   _____

_____   _____

> "Energy follows thought."
> Dan Millman

The Challenge:

_____

_____

_____

_____

_____

_____

_____

_____

_____

_____

_____

_____

_____

_____

_____

_____

Now What?

_____

_____

_____

_____

_____

_____

_____

_____

_____

_____

_____

_____

_____

_____

_____

_____

"If you chase two rabbits,
they both get away."
Anonymous

The Challenge:

Now What?

_____

_____

_____

_____

_____

_____

_____

_____

_____

_____

_____

_____

_____

_____

_____

_____

_____

_____

_____

_____

_____

_____

_____

_____

_____

_____

_____

_____

_____

_____

"Never make a decision out of
fear."
Joseph Filice

The Challenge:

_____

_____

_____

_____

_____

_____

Now What?

_____

_____

> "Never let a fat person tell you
> how to lose weight."
> Author, Gino Pomilia

The Challenge:

_____

_____

_____

_____

_____

_____

_____

_____

_____

_____

_____

_____

_____

_____

Now What?

_____

_____

_____

_____

_____

_____

_____

_____

_____

_____

_____

_____

_____

_____

_____

_____

"Do what is right, not what is easy."
Roy T. Bennett

The Challenge:

_____

_____

_____

_____

_____

_____

_____

_____

_____

_____

_____

_____

_____

_____

_____

_____

Now What?

_____

_____

_____

_____

_____

_____

_____

_____

_____

_____

_____

_____

_____

_____

_____

"Don't underestimate the
importance of 'It's Possible.'"
Unknown

The Challenge:

Now What?

_____

_____

_____

_____

_____

_____

_____

_____

_____

_____

_____

_____

_____

_____

_____

_____

> "Work hard in silence; let your
> success be your noise."
> Frank Ocean

The Challenge:

_____

_____

_____

_____

_____

_____

_____

_____

_____

_____

_____

_____

_____

_____

_____

Now What?

_____

_____

_____

_____

_____

_____

_____

_____

_____

_____

_____

_____

_____

_____

_____

"If you compromise who you are for anyone or anything, you can never be the person you want to be."
Unknown

The Challenge:

_____

_____

_____

_____

_____

_____

_____

_____

_____

_____

_____

_____

_____

Now What?

_____

_____

_____

_____

_____

_____

_____

_____

_____

_____

_____

_____

_____

_____

_____

_____

"You'll eventually define yourself
by what you do consistently, not by
what you say."
Aristotle

The Challenge:

_____

_____

_____

_____

_____

_____

_____

_____

_____

_____

_____

_____

_____

_____

_____

_____

Now What?

_____

_____

_____

_____

_____

_____

_____

_____

_____

_____

_____

_____

_____

_____

_____

_____

_____

> "I'm a slow walker, but I never walk backward."
> Abraham Lincoln

The Challenge:

_____

_____

_____

_____

_____

_____

_____

_____

_____

_____

_____

_____

_____

_____

_____

Now What?

_____

_____

_____

_____

_____

_____

_____

_____

_____

_____

_____

_____

_____

_____

_____

_____

"It's no use in saying 'I am doing my best'. You must succeed in doing what is necessary."
Winston Churchill

The Challenge:

_____

_____

_____

_____

_____

_____

_____

_____

_____

_____

_____

_____

_____

_____

Now What?

_____

_____

_____

_____

_____

_____

_____

_____

_____

_____

_____

_____

_____

_____

"When you want to attempt a personal challenge, NEVER worry about what others may think. Remember, you're not doing it for them."
Author, Gino Pomilia

The Challenge:

_____

_____

_____

_____

_____

_____

_____

_____

_____

_____

_____

_____

_____

_____

Now What?

_____

_____

_____

_____

_____

_____

_____

_____

_____

_____

_____

_____

_____

_____

_____

_____

"Remember; even in silence,
you take a stand."
Pope John Paul II

The Challenge:

_____

_____

_____

_____

_____

_____

_____

_____

_____

_____

_____

_____

_____

_____

_____

Now What?

_____

_____

_____

_____

_____

_____

_____

_____

_____

_____

_____

_____

_____

_____

_____

"Never let one person's opinion of you dictate who you are or what you can do."
Les Brown

The Challenge:

_____

_____

_____

_____

_____

_____

_____

_____

_____

_____

_____

_____

_____

Now What?

_____

_____

_____

_____

_____

_____

_____

_____

_____

_____

_____

_____

_____

_____

_____

> "Habits die hard, so make your
> habits good habits."
> Coach Al Endriss

The Challenge:

_____

_____

_____

_____

_____

_____

_____

_____

_____

_____

_____

_____

_____

_____

Now What?

_____

_____

_____

_____

_____

_____

_____

_____

_____

_____

_____

_____

_____

_____

_____

"The harder you work, the harder it
is to surrender."
Rocky Marciano

The Challenge:

Now What?

_____

_____

_____

_____

_____

_____

_____

_____

_____

_____

_____

_____

_____

_____

_____

_____

_____

_____

_____

_____

_____

_____

_____

_____

_____

_____

_____

_____

_____

_____

_____

_____

_____

"No one can wipe their feet on you,
unless you lie down."
My mother, Gloria

The Challenge:

_____

_____

_____

_____

_____

_____

_____

_____

_____

_____

_____

_____

_____

_____

Now What?

_____

_____

_____

_____

_____

_____

_____

_____

_____

_____

_____

_____

_____

_____

_____

"It's easier to swim with the 'tide' than against it, but you end up going where others take you. Going against the 'tide' is what makes us stronger. Soon, not only does the challenge get easier, but you'll find others following you."
Author, Gino Pomilia

The Challenge:

_____

_____

_____

_____

_____

_____

_____

_____

_____

_____

_____

_____

Now What?

_____

_____

_____

_____

_____

_____

_____

_____

_____

_____

_____

_____

_____

_____

"Never give up. As long as you are still alive, your story is not over."
Sylvester Stallone

The Challenge:

_____

_____

_____

_____

_____

_____

_____

_____

_____

_____

_____

_____

_____

_____

Now What?

_____

_____

_____

_____

_____

_____

_____

_____

_____

_____

_____

_____

_____

_____

"Sometimes we are hurt but not surprised."
Timmy Nowell

The Challenge:

_____

_____

_____

_____

_____

_____

_____

_____

_____

_____

_____

_____

_____

_____

Now What?

_____

_____

_____

_____

_____

_____

_____

_____

_____

_____

_____

_____

_____

_____

_____

"Great minds find solutions.
Weak minds find excuses."
Author, Gino Pomilia

The Challenge:

_____

_____

_____

_____

_____

_____

_____

_____

_____

_____

_____

_____

_____

_____

Now What?

_____

_____

_____

_____

_____

_____

_____

_____

_____

_____

_____

_____

_____

_____

"It ain't about how hard you hit. It's about how hard you get hit and keep moving forward; how much you can take and keep moving forward. That's how winning is done."
Rocky Balboa

The Challenge:

_____

_____

_____

_____

_____

_____

_____

_____

_____

_____

_____

_____

Now What?

_____

_____

_____

_____

_____

_____

_____

_____

_____

_____

_____

_____

_____

_____

"Many times, we never realize our opportunities when they're right in front of us."
Author, Gino Pomilia

The Challenge:

_____

_____

_____

_____

_____

_____

_____

_____

_____

_____

_____

_____

_____

_____

Now What?

_____

_____

_____

_____

_____

_____

_____

_____

_____

_____

_____

_____

_____

_____

> "The degree to which you believe good things can happen is the degree to which your work will be effective."
> Therapist Ben

The Challenge:

_____

_____

_____

_____

_____

_____

_____

_____

_____

_____

_____

_____

_____

Now What?

_____

_____

_____

_____

_____

_____

_____

_____

_____

_____

_____

_____

_____

_____

_____

"No matter what you lose in life,
never lose yourself."
My mother, Gloria

The Challenge:

_____

_____

_____

_____

_____

_____

_____

_____

_____

_____

_____

_____

_____

_____

Now What?

_____

_____

_____

_____

_____

_____

_____

_____

_____

_____

_____

_____

_____

_____

"It isn't the mountains ahead that wear you out; it's the pebble in your shoe."
Muhammad Ali

The Challenge:

_____

_____

_____

_____

_____

_____

_____

_____

_____

_____

_____

_____

_____

_____

Now What?

_____

_____

_____

_____

_____

_____

_____

_____

_____

_____

_____

_____

_____

_____

"The two most important days in
your life are the day you are born
and the day you find out why."
Mark Twain

The Challenge:

_____

_____

_____

_____

_____

_____

_____

_____

_____

_____

_____

_____

_____

_____

_____

Now What?

_____

_____

_____

_____

_____

_____

_____

_____

_____

_____

_____

_____

_____

_____

_____

"When we are drowning,
sometimes we describe the water,
instead of learning how to swim."
Jack Nicholson, "As Good as It Gets."

The Challenge:

_____

_____

_____

_____

_____

_____

_____

_____

_____

_____

_____

_____

_____

_____

Now What?

_____

_____

_____

_____

_____

_____

_____

_____

_____

_____

_____

_____

_____

_____

_____

"Every day, somebody somewhere accomplishes something that they've never accomplished before. Why can't that somebody be you today?"
Coach Al Endriss

The Challenge:

_____

_____

_____

_____

_____

_____

_____

_____

_____

_____

_____

_____

_____

Now What?

_____

_____

_____

_____

_____

_____

_____

_____

_____

_____

_____

_____

_____

"Shit happens in every language."
Unknown

The Challenge:

_____

_____

_____

_____

_____

_____

_____

_____

_____

_____

_____

_____

_____

_____

_____

Now What?

_____

_____

_____

_____

_____

_____

_____

_____

_____

_____

_____

_____

_____

_____

_____

_____

> "If you don't say anything, you can't say the wrong thing."
> Author, Gino Pomilia

The Challenge:

_____

_____

_____

_____

_____

_____

_____

_____

_____

_____

_____

_____

_____

_____

Now What?

_____

_____

_____

_____

_____

_____

_____

_____

_____

_____

_____

_____

_____

_____

The Challenge:

_____

_____

_____

_____

_____

_____

_____

_____

_____

_____

_____

_____

_____

_____

_____

Now What?

_____

_____

_____

_____

_____

_____

_____

_____

_____

_____

_____

_____

_____

_____

_____

_____

"There are two ways of being fooled. One is to believe what isn't true; the other is to refuse to believe what is true."
Danish philosopher Søren Kierkegaard

The Challenge:

_____

_____

_____

_____

_____

_____

_____

_____

_____

_____

_____

_____

_____

Now What?

_____

_____

_____

_____

_____

_____

_____

_____

_____

_____

_____

_____

_____

_____

"There comes a point in your life when you realize who matters, who never did, and who always will."
Adam Lindsay Gordon

The Challenge:

_____

_____

_____

_____

_____

_____

_____

_____

_____

_____

_____

_____

_____

_____

_____

Now What?

_____

_____

_____

_____

_____

_____

_____

_____

_____

_____

_____

_____

_____

_____

_____

_____

"Sometimes you have to let go of the picture of what you thought life would be like and learn to find joy in the story you're living."
Rachel Marie Martin

The Challenge:

_____

_____

_____

_____

_____

_____

_____

_____

_____

_____

_____

_____

Now What?

_____

_____

_____

_____

_____

_____

_____

_____

_____

_____

_____

_____

> "The older I get, the less I care about what people think of me. Therefore, the older I get, the more I enjoy life."
> Oscar Auliq-Ice

The Challenge:

_____

_____

_____

_____

_____

_____

_____

_____

_____

_____

_____

_____

_____

_____

Now What?

_____

_____

_____

_____

_____

_____

_____

_____

_____

_____

_____

_____

_____

_____

"Worrying does not take away
tomorrow's troubles.
It takes away today's peace."
Randy Armstrong

The Challenge:

_____

_____

_____

_____

_____

_____

_____

_____

_____

_____

_____

_____

_____

_____

Now What?

_____

_____

_____

_____

_____

_____

_____

_____

_____

_____

_____

_____

_____

_____

"Everything you do either gets you closer to or farther from your goals."
Buddy Biancalana

The Challenge:

_____

_____

_____

_____

_____

_____

_____

_____

_____

_____

_____

_____

_____

_____

Now What?

_____

_____

_____

_____

_____

_____

_____

_____

_____

_____

_____

_____

_____

_____

_____

_____

"In a time of stress, you will revert back to what you know best."
Coach Al Endriss

The Challenge:

Now What?

_____

_____

_____

_____

_____

_____

_____

_____

_____

_____

_____

_____

_____

_____

_____

_____

_____

"My 'To-Do' list:
Count my blessings, practice kindness, let go of what I can't control, listen to my heart, be productive yet calm."
Unknown

The Challenge:

_____

_____

_____

_____

_____

_____

_____

_____

_____

_____

_____

_____

_____

Now What?

_____

_____

_____

_____

_____

_____

_____

_____

_____

_____

_____

_____

_____

"Every failure is a lesson. If you are not willing to fail, you are not ready to succeed."
Ken Robinson

The Challenge:

Now What?

_____

_____

_____

> "Pain will eventually subside, but glory lasts forever."
> Unknown

The Challenge:

_____

_____

_____

_____

_____

_____

_____

_____

_____

_____

_____

_____

_____

_____

Now What?

_____

_____

_____

_____

_____

_____

_____

_____

_____

_____

_____

_____

_____

_____

_____

"Everybody learns in life; it's just how quickly you learn that will determine how far you go in life."
John Wooden, Harry Truman, & Earl Weaver

The Challenge:

_____

_____

_____

_____

_____

_____

_____

_____

_____

_____

_____

_____

_____

_____

Now What?

_____

_____

_____

_____

_____

_____

_____

_____

_____

_____

_____

_____

_____

_____

_____

"Remember that guy who gave up?
Neither does anybody else."
Ashton Kutcher

The Challenge:

_____

_____

_____

_____

_____

_____

_____

_____

_____

_____

_____

_____

_____

_____

Now What?

_____

_____

_____

_____

_____

_____

_____

_____

_____

_____

_____

_____

_____

_____

_____

"The brave may not live forever,
but the timid do not live at all."
Richard Branson

The Challenge:

Now What?

_____

_____

_____

_____

_____

_____

_____

_____

_____

_____

_____

_____

_____

_____

_____

_____

_____

_____

_____

_____

_____

_____

_____

_____

_____

_____

_____

_____

_____

_____

> "The truth is like a lion. You don't need to defend it. Let it loose, and it will defend itself."
> Saint Augustine

The Challenge:

_____

_____

_____

_____

_____

_____

_____

_____

_____

_____

_____

_____

_____

Now What?

_____

_____

_____

_____

_____

_____

_____

_____

_____

_____

_____

_____

_____

_____

_____

"Your time is limited. Don't
waste it living someone else's life."
Steve Jobs

The Challenge:

_____

_____

_____

_____

_____

_____

_____

_____

_____

_____

_____

_____

_____

_____

Now What?

_____

_____

_____

_____

_____

_____

_____

_____

_____

_____

_____

_____

_____

_____

> "Fear does not stop death.
> It stops life."
> Vi Keeland & Naguib Mahfouz

The Challenge:

_____

_____

_____

_____

_____

_____

_____

_____

_____

_____

_____

_____

_____

_____

Now What?

_____

_____

_____

_____

_____

_____

_____

_____

_____

_____

_____

_____

_____

_____

_____

_____

"Sometimes God closes doors because it's time to move forward. He knows you won't move unless your circumstances force you."
Christine Caine

The Challenge:

_____

_____

_____

_____

_____

_____

_____

_____

_____

_____

_____

_____

_____

Now What?

_____

_____

_____

_____

_____

_____

_____

_____

_____

_____

_____

_____

_____

"Live simply. Love generously. Care deeply. Speak kindly. Leave the rest to God."
Ronald Reagan

The Challenge:

_____

_____

_____

_____

_____

_____

_____

_____

_____

_____

_____

_____

_____

_____

Now What?

_____

_____

_____

_____

_____

_____

_____

_____

_____

_____

_____

_____

_____

_____

> "Don't let someone who has nothing tell you how to do anything."
> Wayne W. Johnson

The Challenge:

_____

_____

_____

_____

_____

_____

_____

_____

_____

_____

_____

_____

_____

_____

Now What?

_____

_____

_____

_____

_____

_____

_____

_____

_____

_____

_____

_____

_____

_____

_____

> "The biggest troublemaker you'll probably ever have to deal with watches you from the mirror every morning."
> An old farmer's advice

The Challenge:

_____

_____

_____

_____

_____

_____

_____

_____

_____

_____

_____

_____

_____

Now What?

_____

_____

_____

_____

_____

_____

_____

_____

_____

_____

_____

_____

_____

_____

_____

"I have been broken. I have known hardships, and I have lost myself. But here I stand, still moving forward and growing stronger each day. I will never forget the harsh lessons in my life. They made me stronger."
Unknown

The Challenge:

_____

_____

_____

_____

_____

_____

_____

_____

_____

_____

_____

Now What?

_____

_____

_____

_____

_____

_____

_____

_____

_____

_____

_____

_____

> "The biggest mistake I have made in my life is letting people stay in my life far longer than they deserve."
> Steven Wandel

The Challenge:

_____

_____

_____

_____

_____

_____

_____

_____

_____

_____

_____

_____

_____

_____

Now What?

_____

_____

_____

_____

_____

_____

_____

_____

_____

_____

_____

_____

_____

_____

_____

> "Timing has a lot to do with
> the outcome of a rain dance."
> Texas Bix Bender

The Challenge:

_____

_____

_____

_____

_____

_____

_____

_____

_____

_____

_____

_____

_____

_____

_____

Now What?

_____

_____

_____

_____

_____

_____

_____

_____

_____

_____

_____

_____

_____

_____

_____

> "Pain is temporary,
> but quitting lasts forever."
> Lance Armstrong

The Challenge:

_____

_____

_____

_____

_____

_____

_____

_____

_____

_____

_____

_____

_____

_____

Now What?

_____

_____

_____

_____

_____

_____

_____

_____

_____

_____

_____

_____

_____

_____

_____

_____

> "Don't interfere with something
> that ain't bothering you."
> Old Farmer Wisdom

The Challenge:

_____

_____

_____

_____

_____

_____

_____

_____

_____

_____

_____

_____

_____

_____

_____

Now What?

_____

_____

_____

_____

_____

_____

_____

_____

_____

_____

_____

_____

_____

_____

_____

"Live a good, honorable life. Then when you get older and think back, you'll enjoy it a second time."
The Dalai Lama

The Challenge:

_____

_____

_____

_____

_____

_____

_____

_____

_____

_____

_____

_____

_____

_____

_____

Now What?

_____

_____

_____

_____

_____

_____

_____

_____

_____

_____

_____

_____

_____

_____

_____

> "Remember that silence is
> sometimes the best answer."
> Dalai Lama XIV

The Challenge:

_____

_____

_____

_____

_____

_____

_____

_____

_____

_____

_____

_____

_____

_____

_____

Now What?

_____

_____

_____

_____

_____

_____

_____

_____

_____

_____

_____

_____

_____

_____

_____

"The best sermons are lived,
not preached."
Pastor Tim Burt

The Challenge:

_____

_____

_____

_____

_____

_____

_____

_____

_____

_____

_____

_____

_____

_____

Now What?

_____

_____

_____

_____

_____

_____

_____

_____

_____

_____

_____

_____

_____

_____

_____

> "Some people create their own storms, then get upset when it rains."
> Unknown

The Challenge:

_____

_____

_____

_____

_____

_____

_____

_____

_____

_____

_____

_____

_____

Now What?

_____

_____

_____

_____

_____

_____

_____

_____

_____

_____

_____

_____

_____

_____

_____

> "Life is simpler when you plow around the stump."
> Old Farmer Advice

The Challenge:

_____

_____

_____

_____

_____

_____

_____

_____

_____

_____

_____

_____

_____

Now What?

_____

_____

_____

_____

_____

_____

_____

_____

_____

_____

_____

_____

_____

_____

"Never underestimate your ability to change or overestimate your ability to change others."
Peggy Stewart

The Challenge:

_____

_____

_____

_____

_____

_____

_____

_____

_____

_____

_____

_____

_____

_____

Now What?

_____

_____

_____

_____

_____

_____

_____

_____

_____

_____

_____

_____

_____

_____

> "No amount of money ever bought a second of time."
> Tony Stark, Iron Man

The Challenge:

_____

_____

_____

_____

_____

_____

_____

_____

_____

_____

_____

_____

_____

_____

Now What?

_____

_____

_____

_____

_____

_____

_____

_____

_____

_____

_____

_____

_____

_____

_____

"Surround yourself with people
who see your value and
remind you of it."
Brad Sharp

The Challenge:

_____

_____

_____

_____

_____

_____

_____

_____

_____

_____

_____

_____

_____

_____

_____

Now What?

_____

_____

_____

_____

_____

_____

_____

_____

_____

_____

_____

_____

_____

_____

_____

_____

> "Our dreams belong to us. A life without dreams is no life at all."
> Langston Hughes

The Challenge:

_____

_____

_____

_____

_____

_____

_____

_____

_____

_____

_____

_____

_____

_____

_____

Now What?

_____

_____

_____

_____

_____

_____

_____

_____

_____

_____

_____

_____

_____

_____

_____

"Remember, life may lead you where you least expect, but have faith that you are exactly where you are meant to be."
Talon, Snow Buddies

The Challenge:

_____

_____

_____

_____

_____

_____

_____

_____

_____

_____

_____

_____

_____

_____

Now What?

_____

_____

_____

_____

_____

_____

_____

_____

_____

_____

_____

_____

_____

_____

_____

"People reveal themselves
through their actions."
Maya Angelou

The Challenge:

_____

_____

_____

_____

_____

_____

_____

_____

_____

_____

_____

_____

_____

_____

_____

Now What?

_____

_____

_____

_____

_____

_____

_____

_____

_____

_____

_____

_____

_____

_____

_____

_____

"Admire those who attempt great things, even though they may fail."
Roman Philosopher Seneca

The Challenge:

_____

_____

_____

_____

_____

_____

_____

_____

_____

_____

_____

_____

_____

_____

_____

_____

Now What?

_____

_____

_____

_____

_____

_____

_____

_____

_____

_____

_____

_____

_____

_____

_____

_____

> "Doubt kills more dreams than
> failure ever will."
> Suzy Kassem

The Challenge:

_____

_____

_____

_____

_____

_____

_____

_____

_____

_____

_____

_____

_____

_____

Now What?

_____

_____

_____

_____

_____

_____

_____

_____

_____

_____

_____

_____

_____

_____

_____

"Don't stop when you're tired.
Stop when you're done."
Marilyn Monroe & David Goggins

The Challenge:

_____

_____

_____

_____

_____

_____

_____

_____

_____

_____

_____

_____

_____

_____

_____

Now What?

_____

_____

_____

_____

_____

_____

_____

_____

_____

_____

_____

_____

_____

_____

_____

"You cannot hang out with negative people and expect to live a positive life."
Joel Osteen

The Challenge:

_____
_____
_____
_____
_____
_____
_____
_____
_____
_____
_____
_____
_____

Now What?

_____
_____
_____
_____
_____
_____
_____
_____
_____
_____
_____
_____
_____
_____
_____
_____

> "Believe you can, and you're halfway there."
> Theodore Roosevelt

The Challenge:

_____

_____

_____

_____

_____

_____

_____

_____

_____

_____

_____

_____

_____

_____

_____

_____

Now What?

_____

_____

_____

_____

_____

_____

_____

_____

_____

_____

_____

_____

_____

_____

_____

_____

> "One day you will thank yourself
> for never giving up."
> Anonymous

The Challenge:

Now What?

_____

_____

_____

_____

_____

_____

_____

_____

_____

_____

_____

_____

_____

_____

_____

_____

> "Lessons in life are repeated,
> until they are learned."
> Frank Sonnenberg

The Challenge:

_____

_____

_____

_____

_____

_____

_____

_____

_____

_____

_____

_____

_____

_____

Now What?

_____

_____

_____

_____

_____

_____

_____

_____

_____

_____

_____

_____

_____

_____

"Stop letting people who do little for you, control so much of your mind, feelings, and emotions."
Will Smith

The Challenge:

Now What?

_____

_____

_____

_____

_____

_____

_____

_____

_____

_____

_____

_____

_____

_____

_____

> "The harder you work,
> the luckier you get."
> Thomas Jefferson & Gary Player

The Challenge:

_____

_____

_____

_____

_____

_____

_____

_____

_____

_____

_____

_____

_____

_____

Now What?

_____

_____

_____

_____

_____

_____

_____

_____

_____

_____

_____

_____

_____

_____

_____

> "Fear doesn't exist, except in your mind."
> Dale Carnegie

The Challenge:

_____

_____

_____

_____

_____

_____

_____

_____

_____

_____

_____

_____

_____

_____

_____

Now What?

_____

_____

_____

_____

_____

_____

_____

_____

_____

_____

_____

_____

_____

_____

_____

_____

_____

> "If people aren't calling you crazy,
> you aren't thinking big enough."
> Richard Branson

The Challenge:

_____

_____

_____

_____

_____

_____

_____

_____

_____

_____

_____

_____

_____

_____

_____

Now What?

_____

_____

_____

_____

_____

_____

_____

_____

_____

_____

_____

_____

_____

_____

_____

"You must expect great things of
yourself before you can do them."
Michael Jordan

The Challenge:

_____

_____

_____

_____

_____

_____

_____

_____

_____

_____

_____

_____

_____

_____

_____

Now What?

_____

_____

_____

_____

_____

_____

_____

_____

_____

_____

_____

_____

_____

_____

_____

_____

"Sometimes later becomes never.
Do it now."
Anonymous

The Challenge:

_____

_____

_____

_____

_____

_____

_____

_____

_____

_____

_____

_____

_____

_____

_____

_____

_____

Now What?

_____

_____

_____

_____

_____

_____

_____

_____

_____

_____

_____

_____

_____

_____

_____

_____

_____

"Dream Big. Dare to Fail."
Norman Vaughan

The Challenge:

Now What?

_____

_____

_____

_____

_____

_____

_____

_____

_____

_____

_____

_____

_____

_____

_____

_____

"Falling down is an accident.
Staying down is a choice."
Rosemary Nonny Knight

The Challenge:

_____

_____

_____

_____

_____

_____

_____

_____

_____

_____

_____

_____

_____

_____

_____

_____

Now What?

_____

_____

_____

_____

_____

_____

_____

_____

_____

_____

_____

_____

_____

_____

_____

_____

"Don't ever blame what you do or don't do on anyone or anything else. Take responsibility for your own life."
Uncle Frank Pomilia

The Challenge:

_____

_____

_____

_____

_____

_____

_____

_____

_____

_____

_____

_____

_____

_____

Now What?

_____

_____

_____

_____

_____

_____

_____

_____

_____

_____

_____

_____

_____

_____

_____

"Don't take criticism from someone you would never go to for advice."
Morgan Freeman

The Challenge:

_____

_____

_____

_____

_____

_____

_____

_____

_____

_____

_____

_____

_____

_____

_____

_____

Now What?

_____

_____

_____

_____

_____

_____

_____

_____

_____

_____

_____

_____

_____

_____

_____

_____

"Enjoy the process of your search without succumbing to the pressure of the result. Trust your gut."
Will Ferrell

The Challenge:

_____

Now What?

_____

> "Everyone deserves second
> chances, but not
> for the same mistakes."
> Paulo Coelho

The Challenge:

_____

_____

_____

_____

_____

_____

_____

_____

_____

_____

_____

_____

_____

Now What?

_____

_____

_____

_____

_____

_____

_____

_____

_____

_____

_____

_____

_____

_____

"You do stupid things; you
win stupid prizes."
Candace Owens

The Challenge:

Now What?

_____

_____

_____

_____

_____

_____

_____

_____

_____

_____

_____

_____

_____

_____

_____

_____

_____

"Don't fear failure. Fear being in the same place next year as you are today."
Michael Hyatt

The Challenge:

_____

_____

_____

_____

_____

_____

_____

_____

_____

_____

_____

_____

_____

_____

_____

Now What?

_____

_____

_____

_____

_____

_____

_____

_____

_____

_____

_____

_____

_____

_____

_____

"Most people live in fear because they project the past into the future."
Michael Jordan

The Challenge:

Now What?

_____

_____

_____

_____

_____

_____

_____

_____

_____

_____

_____

_____

_____

_____

_____

_____

_____

_____

_____

_____

_____

_____

_____

_____

_____

_____

_____

_____

> "It's never too late to do the
> right thing."
> Nelson Mandela

The Challenge:

_____

_____

_____

_____

_____

_____

_____

_____

_____

_____

_____

_____

_____

_____

Now What?

_____

_____

_____

_____

_____

_____

_____

_____

_____

_____

_____

_____

_____

_____

> "Pain doesn't show up in our lives for no reason. It's a sign that something in our lives needs to change."
> Mandy Hale

The Challenge:

_____

_____

_____

_____

_____

_____

_____

_____

_____

_____

_____

_____

_____

Now What?

_____

_____

_____

_____

_____

_____

_____

_____

_____

_____

_____

_____

_____

_____

_____

_____

"Be careful about what you say about yourself. You will believe everything you hear yourself say, so be positive."
Author, Gino Pomilia

The Challenge:

_____

_____

_____

_____

_____

_____

_____

_____

_____

_____

_____

_____

_____

_____

Now What?

_____

_____

_____

_____

_____

_____

_____

_____

_____

_____

_____

_____

_____

_____

_____

"Not all storms come to disrupt your
life. Some come to clear the path."
The Book of Zahir

The Challenge:

_____

_____

_____

_____

_____

_____

_____

_____

_____

_____

_____

_____

_____

_____

Now What?

_____

_____

_____

_____

_____

_____

_____

_____

_____

_____

_____

_____

_____

_____

_____

"Failure is nothing more than a
chance to revise your strategy."
Lauren Patrick

The Challenge:

_____

_____

_____

_____

_____

_____

_____

_____

_____

_____

_____

_____

_____

Now What?

_____

_____

_____

_____

_____

_____

_____

_____

_____

_____

_____

_____

_____

"When you attempt something, your success or failure only defines the moment, not the person."
Thomas Edison

The Challenge:

_____

_____

_____

_____

_____

_____

_____

_____

_____

_____

_____

_____

_____

Now What?

_____

_____

_____

_____

_____

_____

_____

_____

_____

_____

_____

_____

_____

_____

_____

_____

"In the END, it's not the years in your life that count, but it's the life in your years."
Possibly, Abraham Lincoln

The Challenge:

_____

_____

_____

_____

_____

_____

_____

_____

_____

_____

_____

_____

_____

_____

_____

Now What?

_____

_____

_____

_____

_____

_____

_____

_____

_____

_____

_____

_____

_____

_____

_____

_____

_____

"It is not death that a man should fear, but he should fear never beginning to live."
Marcus Aurelius

The Challenge:

_____

_____

_____

_____

_____

_____

_____

_____

_____

_____

_____

_____

_____

Now What?

_____

_____

_____

_____

_____

_____

_____

_____

_____

_____

_____

_____

_____

_____

"No one can rewrite the past. We can, however, write a new beginning."
Author, Gino Pomilia

The Challenge:

_____
_____
_____
_____
_____
_____
_____
_____
_____
_____
_____
_____
_____
_____
_____

Now What?

_____
_____
_____
_____
_____
_____
_____
_____
_____
_____
_____
_____
_____
_____
_____

> "Great things never came from comfort zones."
> Neil Stress & Roy T. Bennett

The Challenge:

_____

_____

_____

_____

_____

_____

_____

_____

_____

_____

_____

_____

_____

_____

Now What?

_____

_____

_____

_____

_____

_____

_____

_____

_____

_____

_____

_____

_____

_____

_____

_____

"Sometimes you have to get knocked down lower than you have ever been to stand back up taller than you ever were."
Unknown

The Challenge:

_____

_____

_____

_____

_____

_____

_____

_____

_____

_____

_____

_____

_____

_____

_____

Now What?

_____

_____

_____

_____

_____

_____

_____

_____

_____

_____

_____

_____

_____

_____

_____

_____

"Dreams can only work if you do."
John C. Maxwell

The Challenge:

Now What?

_____

_____

_____

_____

_____

_____

_____

_____

_____

_____

_____

_____

_____

_____

_____

> "Don't expect to see a change
> if you don't make one."
> Unknown

The Challenge:

Now What?

_____

_____

_____

_____

_____

_____

_____

_____

_____

_____

_____

_____

_____

_____

_____

_____

_____

"Hope is seeing light despite
being surrounded by darkness."
Desmond Tutu

The Challenge:

Now What?

_____

_____

_____

_____

_____

_____

_____

_____

_____

_____

_____

_____

_____

_____

_____

_____

_____

_____

"When you change the way you look at things, the things you look at change."
Dr. Wayne Dyer

The Challenge:

_____

_____

_____

_____

_____

_____

_____

_____

_____

_____

_____

_____

_____

_____

Now What?

_____

_____

_____

_____

_____

_____

_____

_____

_____

_____

_____

_____

_____

_____

_____

The more you believe, the more you will change, and the more you change, the better you will feel."
Therapist Ben

The Challenge:

_____

_____

_____

_____

_____

_____

_____

_____

_____

_____

_____

_____

_____

Now What?

_____

_____

_____

_____

_____

_____

_____

_____

_____

_____

_____

_____

_____

_____

_____

> "It may be hard, but hard is not impossible."
> Denzel Washington

The Challenge:

_____

_____

_____

_____

_____

_____

_____

_____

_____

_____

_____

_____

_____

_____

Now What?

_____

_____

_____

_____

_____

_____

_____

_____

_____

_____

_____

_____

_____

_____

"Never be a prisoner of your past.
It was a lesson, not a life sentence."
Unknown

The Challenge:

Now What?

_____

_____

_____

_____

_____

_____

_____

_____

_____

_____

_____

_____

_____

_____

_____

"Don't do something permanently
stupid just because you're
temporarily upset."
Zig Ziglar

The Challenge:

_____

_____

_____

_____

_____

_____

_____

_____

_____

_____

_____

_____

_____

_____

Now What?

_____

_____

_____

_____

_____

_____

_____

_____

_____

_____

_____

_____

_____

_____

_____

"The only thing that overcomes
hard luck is hard work."
Harry Golden

The Challenge:

Now What?

_____

_____

_____

_____

_____

_____

_____

_____

"Many quit without realizing how
close they were to success."
Thomas Edison

The Challenge:

_____

_____

_____

_____

_____

_____

_____

_____

_____

_____

_____

_____

_____

_____

Now What?

_____

_____

_____

_____

_____

_____

_____

_____

_____

_____

_____

_____

_____

_____

> "If you believe it will work out, you'll see opportunities. If you believe it won't, you'll see obstacles."
> Wayne W. Dyer

The Challenge:

_____

_____

_____

_____

_____

_____

_____

_____

_____

_____

_____

_____

_____

_____

_____

Now What?

_____

_____

_____

_____

_____

_____

_____

_____

_____

_____

_____

_____

_____

_____

_____

_____

> "Stop being afraid of what could go wrong and start being excited about what could go right."
> Tony Robbins

The Challenge:

_____

_____

_____

_____

_____

_____

_____

_____

_____

_____

_____

_____

_____

Now What?

_____

_____

_____

_____

_____

_____

_____

_____

_____

_____

_____

_____

_____

_____

_____

> "I've never met a strong person
> with an easy past; be proud of your
> scars and that you're still standing."
> Atticus

The Challenge:

Now What?

_____

_____

_____

_____

_____

_____

_____

_____

_____

_____

_____

_____

_____

_____

_____

_____

_____

_____

_____

_____

_____

_____

_____

_____

_____

_____

"Your beliefs, either positive or negative, helpful or hurtful, largely determine everything you do and how you do it."
Brian Tracy

The Challenge:

_____

_____

_____

_____

_____

_____

_____

_____

_____

_____

_____

_____

_____

_____

Now What?

_____

_____

_____

_____

_____

_____

_____

_____

_____

_____

_____

_____

_____

_____

_____

"Things will only get better,
one positive thought at a time."
Norman Vincent Peale

The Challenge:

_____

_____

_____

_____

_____

_____

_____

_____

_____

_____

_____

_____

_____

_____

_____

Now What?

_____

_____

_____

_____

_____

_____

_____

_____

_____

_____

_____

_____

_____

_____

_____

_____

_____

"If they say 'It's impossible',
remember that it's only impossible
for them, not for you."
Unknown

The Challenge:

Now What?

_____

_____

_____

_____

_____

_____

_____

_____

_____

_____

_____

_____

_____

_____

_____

_____

_____

_____

_____

_____

_____

_____

_____

_____

"Don't let the words of others discourage you or hold you back, whether they're words you're hearing now or from the past."
Kathryn Yarborough

The Challenge:

_____

_____

_____

_____

_____

_____

_____

_____

_____

_____

_____

_____

_____

_____

Now What?

_____

_____

_____

_____

_____

_____

_____

_____

_____

_____

_____

_____

_____

_____

_____

_____

"Don't get discouraged by what you're going through. Your time is coming. Where you are is not where you are going to stay."
Unknown

The Challenge:

_____

_____

_____

_____

_____

_____

_____

_____

_____

_____

_____

_____

_____

_____

Now What?

_____

_____

_____

_____

_____

_____

_____

_____

_____

_____

_____

_____

_____

_____

_____

> "The heaviest burdens that we carry are the thoughts in our heads."
> Dimitris Arabatzidis

The Challenge:

_____

_____

_____

_____

_____

_____

_____

_____

_____

_____

_____

_____

_____

_____

Now What?

_____

_____

_____

_____

_____

_____

_____

_____

_____

_____

_____

_____

_____

_____

> "When you feel like quitting,
> think about why you started."
> Roxanne Jon & John Lemme

The Challenge:

Now What?

_____

_____

_____

_____

_____

_____

_____

_____

_____

_____

_____

_____

_____

_____

_____

_____

_____

_____

_____

_____

_____

_____

_____

_____

_____

_____

_____

_____

_____

_____

"If it doesn't challenge you,
It won't change you."
Fred DeVito

The Challenge:

Now What?

"Life has no remote.
Get up and change it yourself."
Mark A. Cooper

The Challenge:

_____

_____

_____

_____

_____

_____

_____

_____

_____

_____

_____

_____

_____

_____

Now What?

_____

_____

_____

_____

_____

_____

_____

_____

_____

_____

_____

_____

_____

_____

"You can't start the next chapter of your life, if you keep re-reading the last one."
Michael McMillian

The Challenge:

_____

_____

_____

_____

_____

_____

_____

_____

_____

_____

_____

_____

_____

_____

Now What?

_____

_____

_____

_____

_____

_____

_____

_____

_____

_____

_____

_____

_____

_____

_____

"It's hard to beat a person
who never gives up."
Babe Ruth

The Challenge:

Now What?

_____

_____

_____

_____

_____

> "The distance between your
> dreams and reality is called action."
> Brian Tracy

The Challenge:

_____

_____

_____

_____

_____

_____

_____

_____

_____

_____

_____

_____

_____

_____

Now What?

_____

_____

_____

_____

_____

_____

_____

_____

_____

_____

_____

_____

_____

_____

"Whatever you want for tomorrow,
you'd better start working on
today."
Unknown

The Challenge:

_____

_____

_____

_____

_____

_____

_____

_____

_____

_____

_____

_____

_____

_____

Now What?

_____

_____

_____

_____

_____

_____

_____

_____

_____

_____

_____

_____

_____

_____

"The best way to predict your
future is to create it."
Abraham Lincoln

The Challenge:

_____

_____

_____

_____

_____

_____

_____

_____

_____

_____

_____

_____

_____

_____

Now What?

_____

_____

_____

_____

_____

_____

_____

_____

_____

_____

_____

_____

_____

_____

_____

_____

"The best way to get back on your
feet is to get off your ass."
Senator John Kennedy

The Challenge:

_____

_____

_____

_____

_____

_____

_____

_____

_____

_____

_____

_____

_____

_____

Now What?

_____

_____

_____

_____

_____

_____

_____

_____

_____

_____

_____

_____

_____

_____

"Courage is being scared to death, but saddling up anyway."
John Wayne

The Challenge:

_____

_____

_____

_____

_____

_____

_____

_____

_____

_____

_____

_____

_____

_____

Now What?

_____

_____

_____

_____

_____

_____

_____

_____

_____

_____

_____

_____

_____

_____

_____

"Sometimes the RIGHT thing to do
is also the TOUGHEST thing to do."
Author, Gino Pomilia

The Challenge:

_____

_____

_____

_____

_____

_____

_____

_____

_____

_____

_____

_____

_____

_____

Now What?

_____

_____

_____

_____

_____

_____

_____

_____

_____

_____

_____

_____

_____

_____

> "It's not healthy to jump over
> the wrong fence."
> Coach Al Endriss

The Challenge:

_____

_____

_____

_____

_____

_____

_____

_____

_____

_____

_____

_____

_____

_____

_____

Now What?

_____

_____

_____

_____

_____

_____

_____

_____

_____

_____

_____

_____

_____

_____

_____

_____

"The greatest mistake that you can make in life is to continually be afraid that you will make one."
Elbert Hubbards

The Challenge:

Now What?

_____

_____

_____

_____

_____

_____

_____

_____

_____

_____

_____

_____

_____

_____

_____

_____

"Don't ever lose your momentum."
President Donald J. Trump

The Challenge:

Now What?

_____

_____

_____

_____

_____

_____

_____

_____

_____

_____

_____

_____

_____

_____

_____

_____

_____

_____

_____

_____

_____

_____

_____

_____

_____

_____

_____

_____

_____

_____

"Never take 22 steps to go 2 feet."
Author, Gino Pomilia

The Challenge:

_____

_____

_____

_____

_____

_____

_____

_____

_____

_____

_____

_____

_____

_____

_____

_____

_____

Now What?

_____

_____

_____

_____

_____

_____

_____

_____

_____

_____

_____

_____

_____

_____

_____

_____

"Starting today, I need to forget what's gone, appreciate what still remains, and look forward to what's coming next."
Roy "Dusty" Rogers Jr.

The Challenge:

_____

_____

_____

_____

_____

_____

_____

_____

_____

_____

_____

_____

_____

_____

Now What?

_____

_____

_____

_____

_____

_____

_____

_____

_____

_____

_____

_____

_____

_____

_____

_____

www.ingramcontent.com/pod-product-compliance
Lightning Source LLC
Chambersburg PA
CBHW081325120626
46546CB00011B/3226